Fields of the Kingdom
Pastor Tony Bateman

Copyright © 2024 by Charles Bateman

All rights reserved. No part of this book may be reproduced or used in any manner without written permission of the author except for the use of quotations in a book review.

For more information, email canthonybateman@gmail.com.

www.tfieldinglowecompany.com

DEDICATION

To my beloved wife, Shalita,

You are the cornerstone of our family, the guiding light in our lives. Your unwavering love, support, and patience have been the bedrock upon which our dreams and aspirations have flourished. In every moment, you've been my partner, my confidante, and my best friend. Your strength and grace inspire me endlessly, and I am profoundly grateful for your presence in my life.

To my dear sons, Micah and Joshua,

You two are my greatest joys, my proudest achievements. Watching you grow and learn, witnessing your boundless curiosity and infectious laughter, fills my heart with immeasurable happiness. Your love is a constant reminder of life's truest blessings, and I am honored to be your father. May you always pursue your dreams with passion, kindness, and courage.

TABLE OF CONTENTS

Chapter 1	THE FIELD	Page 1
Chapter 2	EXPECTATIONS	Page 6
Chapter 3	WORKING THE FIELD	Page 11
Chapter 4	WAITING	Page 16
Chapter 5	THE HARVEST	Page 21

INTRODUCTION

It is unusual for me to preach a sermon series; up until recently, I had never done so. At age 37, I spent almost 16 years preaching the Gospel, yet I never had to preach a series. One could argue that the opportunity never presented itself for most of my time in ministry, and they would be somewhat correct. I was a youth pastor or associate pastor for the first ten years of ministry. As a youth pastor, I did not have to preach every Sunday. In 2018, my wife and I were installed as lead pastors of Chase City Church of God, located in Chase City, Virginia. Now, to give you some backstory, I was the fourth Pastor in five years at this church, and upon doing so, I quickly found that I was taking over a church with a congregation of only four people. This was not ideal for a 31-year-old father of two, but my wife and I were determined to make the best of it and work in the field God had provided us with.

Over the past four years, we have been blessed to see our congregation increase by over ten times its original number; we have also completed two small renovations to the property and have significantly impacted the community. In 2020, I had the opportunity to meet Pastor Michael Booker from Bristol, Virginia. Pastor Booker and I became instant friends, and he began to show me the value of a sermon series. How ironic it is now that my first-ever sermon series, "Harvest Time, " inspired this book.

CHAPTER 1: THE FIELD

What caused me to dive into this topic and make it into a series was an analysis of Luke 8:5-8 where Jesus delivers what is known as the parable of the Sower. The four verses talk primarily about the seed and the ground it lands on. As I thought about this, I applied it to ministry. As a minister, I have heard much talk about being "Kingdom Minded," and I confess that I consider myself a "Kingdom Minded" pastor. That being said, just because a person is kingdom-minded does not mean they are constantly being effective in the Kingdom.

Over the years, I have learned that the "field" has much to do with the harvest. Having spent time around farmers, I have seen what is involved in their fields. Metaphorically, the field a farmer uses can represent people or entire ministries. Understanding this concept is imperative and must be fully understood before it is possible for the believer to even get to Luke chapter eight.

When a farmer selects a field, the land is often not ready for growing. Trees may need to be cut down, stumps pulled up, and debris moved away. This concept reminds me of *Jeremiah 1:10: See, I have this day set thee over the nations and the kingdoms, to root out, and to pull down, and to destroy, and to throw down, to build, and to plant.*

This scripture highlights the work that takes place behind the scenes. So often, we see a finished product without realizing what had to take place to produce it. In the same way, a farmer has to clear the ground and root out stumps; in ministry, there are times when strongholds must be torn down. I know you want to hear a story about being built up, but we all have things God wants to root out of us before he can plant something in us.

We have to allow God to root out some things that will prevent the growth we seek. I can tell you that ministry operates the same way. A leader must account for where the church is to get a clear picture of where they must go. When I first took over as lead Pastor, the building, which was built in 1970, was outdated. We needed to take steps to modernize our facility. Before this could happen, I had to take some things into account. The first and most apparent was the church finances. While the church was debt-free, there was less than one thousand dollars in the bank. The ideas I wanted to present to the church would have to wait a few months. Our funds increased over the next few months, and I reviewed my ideas with the church leadership. The first project was to give the pulpit a fresh paint job. A combination of black and gray paint covered the old paneling. This created a modern look and set the stage for my next project: adding stage lighting to the pulpit area.

Over the next four months, the sanctuary was given a complete makeover. New paint, new lights, removing knee walls, and replacing the flooring in areas gave the entire building a brand-new look. The energy was different, and everyone could feel it. Even those who did not like it had to recognize that change had come.

When you compare church life to farm life, farmers begin to prep the ground, and they must first break the ground, which is the most challenging part. The breaking process takes time, is hard work, and can be painful and time-consuming, but it is necessary. In ministry, it is the same. There are things within us that need to break at times, and if we don't allow God to break them, no growth will occur.

The breaking period is just as relevant for churches as it is for the individual people inside. Tradition has so often held churches back. The body of Christ has spent decades trapped behind man-made walls that usually lack scriptural support. In this season, I believe God is looking for men and women who will not only allow Him to break things in them but also be vessels willing to break new ground in the Kingdom. For example, the breaking process in a ministry is hard in farming. When traditions begin to get torn down, when barriers are broken, people are almost always made uncomfortable. In these crucial moments, leaders must be strategic and communicate their hearts to the people they lead. I used a clear strategy when I embarked on remodeling the sanctuary.

First, I had to make sure the church was on board with the decision to renovate. The decision to renovate shouldn't just be the pastor's or any one person's idea. It should be a group effort, steered by a committee, to ensure no one person is calling the shots. Churches are communal spaces, and you want everyone to enjoy the changes. Be prepared for some people to complain or disapprove of changes. It is usually impossible to appeal to everyone's preferences. I had to create a realistic budget for the project and allow that budget to guide me as I made decisions. I even created a giving campaign to cover the renovations. The remodeling process may reveal other needs, so ensuring your budget has some flexibility is important.

The last part is that you cannot forget logistical concerns that arise when you're working on a sanctuary — namely, you may not be able to meet there for services until the project is complete. If necessary, look for another place to meet temporarily. If you're doing minor work, you may be able to complete it during the week and still meet in the sanctuary for church on Sunday.

This is just a small example of the work that went into what was, in many ways, a breaking process. You cannot approach ministry with a sledgehammer mentality; people will get hurt. There must be a strategy and a clear plan in the breaking process. This process symbolizes God breaking things in us because He has a plan. The scripture says in Philippians 1:6: Being confident of this very thing, that he which hath begun a good work in you will perform it until the day of Jesus Christ: God desires to finish what he has started with us. We must be willing to allow the breaking process to take place in our lives. Only then will we see growth, and that "next step" will begin.
The next phase for many farmers is the turning over of the soil. This process is done to help create seed beds and release the nutrients in the ground. This process also helps to discover and remove any remaining debris from the breaking process. Although less painful or labor-intensive, this part is just as important. Luke 8:6-7 gives us a clear example of what happens when debris remains in the soil, and the Sower plants the seed anyway.

Some fell upon a rock, which withered away as soon as it sprung up because it lacked moisture. Some fell among thorns, which sprang up with them and choked them.

In this text, the Sower did not clear out the rocks and thorns, which choked off and destroyed the crop. Ministry is a process of change and redirection. Only after we have been broken can change come, and we can be prepared for what God has in store for us.

Change in ministry is not unlike the change in life; it can be difficult. In my early days as a Pastor, I found that what often makes change difficult is that it requires a person to go outside their comfort zone. Leaving a metro area of over 1.7 million people to live and pastoring in a county of less than 50,000 was definitely outside my comfort zone. As a leader, I was forced to become the change I wanted to implement. I had to change some things about myself before I began to introduce change to the ministry. We must allow God to work on us before attempting to work on others. A person must have the "God work on me" mentality before they ask God to "work through them."

NOTES

NOTES

Date:

NOTES

CHAPTER 2: EXPECTATIONS

The definition of expectation is a strong belief that something will happen or be the case in the future. A certain expectation level is involved whenever a farmer or someone in agriculture plants a seed. The first part of the expectation is based on what is sown or planted. A person will not plant cotton and expect corn, tobacco, or beans to sprout. The expectation is directly related to what is sown. A person expects what they put in the ground to return to them.

In Luke 6:38, Jesus confirms this very concept: *"Give, and it shall be given unto you; good measure, pressed down, and shaken together, and running over, shall men give into your bosom. For with the same measure that ye mete withal it shall be measured to you again".* Jesus validates that when someone sows, there will be a return on the investment. In ministry, like agriculture, that return will always be related to what is sown or planted. Our expectations must match our efforts; we can only expect a harvest if we are diligent sowers.

Over the years, I have seen many in the Kingdom focus on reaping. The concept has been preached many times, yet one can only reap if one has first sown. Never in the history of agriculture has a farmer expected a harvest without sowing, without planting his field. We today live in a society that expects things to happen while putting forth little to no effort.
I told my congregation recently that I remember coming as a teenager from football practice; my parents sometimes were still at work. If I were hungry, I would get something from the refrigerator and heat it in the microwave. I had to type in the numbers I wanted to get the food to a specific temperature. In

today's society, children only have to hit one number to get the microwave to heat their food, and most microwaves have pictures of the number of things for them to know what number to hit. My point behind this is that something meant to be fast and efficient has only become faster; we live in a world that is always looking for something to be done as quickly as possible.

If pastoral ministry has taught me anything, I must be committed to a process and not be in a hurry. To fully commit to a process, you have first to trust it. As a Lead Pastor, I felt myself becoming impatient. I was sometimes frustrated with how long things took to happen. My frustration was centered around the fact that I was applying my timeline to the vision God had given me instead of trusting that his will would be accomplished in his time.

Only four members were present when my wife and I arrived at our church. The infrastructure needed to be improved, and the resources were very limited. God's vision was clear, but implementing the necessary changes would take some time. At first, I struggled with the "take some time" aspect. I wanted to run with the vision God had given me, but I soon realized that I needed a team in place first to help me implement the vision. The fact that I had multiple ideas and knew what I wanted to accomplish meant nothing if I needed the infrastructure to execute the plan. During this time, I learned the relationship between my resources and my "reach" as a Pastor.

In Isaiah 59:1, the prophet makes a clear statement; *Behold, the LORD'S hand is not shortened, that it cannot save; neither his ear heavy, that it cannot hear:* This, however, does not apply to you and me as leaders. We do not have an unlimited reach; while it is true that nothing is too hard for God, some things are, in fact, too hard for us. This is especially true when operating strictly on carnal resources. Take, for example, a benevolent need in your community of $1,000. If that comes before a church with an operating budget of $250,000 annually, that is considered a small donation. On the other hand, if that need is presented before a church with less than $5,000 in the bank, it is a different situation that may warrant a different decision. This moment showed me that my resources directly affected my reach as a ministry, and I needed to make sure that there was an understanding among my staff, no matter how few of them there were.

Getting the staff to understand what the ministry could and could not do in that first year went a long way in helping us establish goals. The best way to set goals as a ministry is to list what you want to accomplish but still need to do so. After that list is finalized, review it and determine the timeline. This process will allow you to narrow the focus to obtainable things now. Doing this allows you as a leader to properly asses where your ministry is based on how many of those goals you were able to accomplish.

This process plays out each day in the world of agriculture. A farmer's production is limited by how much land he has to farm, which is limited by the amount of money he has to purchase property. A farmer's expectation is based not on what he puts in the ground but on how much they plant. This concept is crucial to understand when it comes to Kingdom-minded ministry. What we invest and the quantity invested goes a long way in the Kingdom of God.

I know what you are thinking; you think I'm talking about money. What if I told you that money is just a part of a person's investment in the Kingdom? Our churches today are full of people who may know how to write a check but fail to volunteer their time or talents. The Kingdom of God, like every local ministry, requires a total investment, not just the things that are easy or make us comfortable. We have to move past the superficial investments that we make simply because they are convenient and require no real commitment. This reminds me of what Jesus said in Matthew 9:36-38: *But when he saw the multitudes, he was moved with compassion because they fainted and were scattered abroad as sheep having no shepherd. Then saith he unto his disciples, The harvest truly is plenteous, but the laborers are few; Pray ye, therefore, the Lord of the harvest, that he will send forth laborers into his harvest.*

Another factor that historically limited farmers was the number of workers they had. Planting, tending, and harvesting so much land by yourself is difficult. The more laborers a farmer had, the greater the productivity. Today, millions of dollars have been spent replacing the workers with machines. Farmers worldwide have tractors, combines, and other equipment to do the jobs that people used to occupy. These machines are also designed to make the process faster and more efficient.

I wonder if we have yet to adopt this thinking regarding ministry. Have we come to a place where we value efficiency over effectiveness? Has technology influenced the Kingdom so much that we need to remember the value of relationships? One thing is sure: COVID-19 exposed the lack of technology in some churches. The next issue may be that during that time, many were spoiled; they were so comfortable with a "virtual" experience that they lacked a desire for an authentic one. While I value technology in church and as a Pastor, I have seen its purpose. I will never use technology to replace Kingdom-minded people looking for an opportunity to serve.

The reason for this is simple: I will never allow something to replace our efforts in the Kingdom. As a leader, I cannot promote only things that "make it easy." If I do that, then complacency can set in. As I stated at the beginning of the chapter, expectations must match effort. Our efforts will only decrease as a leader if I become complacent or allow my staff to do so. If the ministry you lead or are a part of is going to grow, high standards must be in place. These high standards will bring about high expectations only achieved through maximum effort.

NOTES

Date:

NOTES

Date:

NOTES

Date:

CHAPTER 3: WORKING THE FIELD

Perhaps the most important part of the agricultural process is "the field" itself, or more specifically, what happens in the field. A farmer spends most of their time in the field, and the work there is often challenging. There are days spent tilling the ground, and after that, there is a seed planted, and it comes time to water and fertilize the seeds. This process is not only hard work but imperative to the growth of future crops. This also can be said in the Kingdom of God as the work done in the field, at the grassroots level, can be very difficult.

One of the biggest challenges when a seed begins to grow is making sure you use the correct fertilizer. Fertilizer is designed to assist with growth and help provide extra nutrients where the soil may be deficient. Another part of this process is knowing what fertilizer is needed for your planted seed. Certain crops require things that others don't. Knowing what your crops need allows you to provide the proper nutrients better.

It does not matter if you buy a big bag of fertilizer or a small bag of what is known as "plant food"; they all have an area that tells you what amounts of certain chemicals are in the bag. Knowing what you're putting into the seed or the ground matters, and that concept also applies in ministry. We must be able to discern what some people can handle and what some people cannot. The reason is, just like in the farm field, what is suitable for some people can seriously damage someone else. The amount you use is also crucial; people are a lot like crops, and too much of something can take them out.

This further compounds the work and makes the entire process more difficult. I remember my grandfather telling stories of when he was a teenager in those North Carolina fields. The largest field was one mile squared, and he and his brothers had to haul 100-pound fertilizer bags on their backs. The field had areas below sea level; even though they had piled the rows up high, some roads were only sometimes passable.

When the road flooded, he, his father, and his brothers had to carry the fertilizer to the field beyond a certain point. Undoubtedly, this was backbreaking work for all involved, yet the crops needed to make it. As we work in the fields of the Kingdom, we, too, will face difficult things; however, they are necessary.

Another interesting thing about the fertilization process is that there are two different types of fertilizer. One is called synthetic, and the other is organic. Synthetic fertilizers are best known for being fast-acting and coming in various forms, such as liquid, pellet, granule, and spike. Synthetic fertilizers are water-soluble and can be taken up by plants almost immediately.

While this provides quick nutrients and rapid greening, the color won't last as long as when organically derived fertilizers are used. Consumers must reapply synthetic fertilizers regularly to keep the results from fading. Synthetic fertilizers give plants a quick boost but do little to stimulate soil life, improve soil texture, or improve your soil's long-term fertility. They're highly water-soluble and can leach into waterways.

The quick results of synthetic fertilizers can come at a cost; apply too much, and it may burn your lawn and plants.

When used correctly, fertilizers from organic sources benefit plants and soil and generally won't burn or damage plants. Organically derived fertilizers stimulate beneficial soil microorganisms and improve the structure of the soil. Soil microbes play a key role in converting organic fertilizers into soluble nutrients that plants can absorb at a rate they can use. Organically derived fertilizers often provide the secondary and micronutrients plants need, which are usually absent in synthetic fertilizers. They typically have a lower NPK analysis (nitrogen, phosphorus, potassium) than synthetic fertilizers, but they feed plants much longer. As a result, the impact of organic fertilizers on lawns and plants is usually more subtle. It may take a little longer to see results, but the reward is a lawn that stays greener longer.

All that information may not be relevant to you, especially if you are not a farmer or are into agriculture. With that said, let me break this down further. One of the most popular fertilizer brands in the United States is actually "Miracle-Gro," that's right, the label you have seen for decades inside your local Walmart or Home Depot. The interesting part is that Miracle-Grow is not only fertilizer; it also sells other products. You and I know it so well because it is a brand name.

This same comparison can be made regarding churches or how people select which church they want to attend. Over the years, I have noticed that many people become attached or drawn to a "brand name" type of ministry. The ministry may have specific programs or auxiliaries that they find interesting;

therefore, they are drawn to it almost like a person would be drawn to a social club.

This phenomenon is easily explained. Statistics show that about 35% of the attendees of these large megachurches are ages 21-40. One of the main reasons young married couples attend megachurches is that these churches offer far more social experiences than traditional churches. And that sociability extends to children as well as to adults.

Of course, children's Sunday School classes are the norm, but most megachurches also offer such child-friendly amenities as supervised playgrounds and Mothers' Day Out facilities. Many house their daycare centers. Family nights generally abound, wherein kids and their parents can engage in games, crafts, and other family-oriented activities. Megachurches offer a broad spectrum of small groups, clubs, and programs for members and sometimes the community.

While many of these things are great, I am okay with a large ministry, as I have previously served at one. I do think that some trade Spiritual growth for carnal amenities. In other words, they are more drawn to the "programs" and not the actual elements of ministry; they are not trying to be disciplined but rather entertained. And while the entertainment can be fun and the programs uplifting, some may feel empty over time due to a lack of spiritual substance in their lives.

The reason for this is that there is a lack of authenticity in our churches today. We have become a society that wants something as fast as possible with minimal effort put forth. Perhaps the scariest part is that some Pastors become like farmers with synthetic fertilizer; they look at quick growth and will do whatever it takes to achieve it. The artificial product can burn up the crop or even damage the soil. In today's world, we see so many leaders desperate for growth that they risk damaging people. Even with the best intentions, if one is not careful, you could be pouring something into a person, damaging them. In my time as Pastor, I've learned that what is suitable for one member may not be good for another; this is where discernment comes into play. A good leader must seek God on behalf of his flock to understand what each individual needs. In ministry, painting with a broad brush will not get you very far, and the intangible aspects of that method can quickly become outdated.

In ministry today, we need authenticity; now, more than ever, we need transparent and real leaders. Much like the farmer who uses organic fertilizer, we must give the people something genuine. I have found that people who may know very little about God or scripture can still spot fakeness a mile away. We serve a real God; therefore, we must demonstrate Him real and authentically. As Pastor, I tell my staff that "people do not care how much you know until they know how much you care." This concept plays out much like the organic fertilizer; the growth may not be fast, but it will be steady, and there will not be any adverse effects after. Just like organic fertilizer has more sustainability, so does authentic ministry. Discipline is something that takes time and effort. People are often just like crops; they need time to absorb what's being poured into them, time for certain things to take root, and time to grow. As leaders, we must remember that as we work in the field, we must allow time for growth.

NOTES

Date:

NOTES

NOTES

CHAPTER 4: WAITING

The Bible says in Isaiah 40:31; *"But they that wait upon the Lord shall renew their strength; they shall mount up with wings as eagles; they shall run, not be weary; and they shall walk, and not faint."* Despite that, waiting is the most challenging thing for a believer to do. I think of what it's like to be a farmer; you have invested so much time and effort, yet now all you can do is wait. The farmer waits for the season to change, for a run to come, and for growth to occur. Everything he is waiting on is totally out of his control. Believers face the same thing: so many things are outside our control, and all we can do is wait and trust God. It is no different for those who stand in leadership. Like the farmer, you have invested so much time, energy, and resources; now it's up to God to do the rest.

In chapter two, I spoke about the "microwave generation," the generation that pushes a button and things happen. Consider this when it comes to that generation: they can look at the back of every box or container and see how long the product needs to remain in the microwave. There is no patience at all; there is no "unknown." They know an exact amount of time, hit a button, and boom, it's done. Ministry is the opposite; our walk with God does not work that way. There is no preset amount of time for God, yet how often do we try and apply one?

It has always been mind-blowing to me how we can apply time limits to an eternal God, who clearly states in Revelation 1:8, *"I am the Alpha and Omega, the beginning and the end."* How arrogant it must seem to God when we apply deadlines or ultimatums as if we have some control. How dare we use a deadline for the one who created time itself, who predates the universe and sets the events of our lives in motion with a simple command?

Another factor that makes waiting so hard is not necessarily a lack of patience but a lack of faith. Whenever we are in a situation where we have to wait on God, there is an element of faith that must be activated. The Bible says in the book of Romans that every man is given a "measure of faith." This means that all of us, no matter our background, have a certain amount of faith. The amount of faith it takes sometimes to "wait on God" is often too much for some believers and even some of us as leaders.

I often think of how hard a farmer works and how much effort goes into planting crops and tending fields. All of this, however, is subject to the rain that God provides. Even in modern times with irrigation systems, rain is still the number one water source in agriculture. Rain is the number one thing that a farmer cannot control, and no matter how much work they do, it is all dependent on the rain.

In ministry, there are certain things that, as a leader, you cannot control. Whether or not people show up, how often they tithe if they participate in certain events, or volunteer. All of these things are examples of what you cannot control. The only thing you fully control as a leader is your investment, how much you invest in the ministry and the people there. We cannot control how people respond or their feelings toward us. The most challenging part of ministry sometimes is waiting for our investment to produce fruit in people's lives. I can think of many situations where leaders get impatient with people and give up on them. They become convinced that the seeds they planted have been either washed away or choked out by life. I have been there and questioned whether or not the investment I was making would ever return. I asked myself, "is this field really good ground"? Am I wasting my time?

We are never wasting our time when we invest in others. As leaders, our reward comes from seeing the investment return and the blessings God bestows on us for being willing to sow. The biggest mistake many believers make is that they expect the return or the blessing to be directly related to where they have planted or who they sowed into. With God, however, it does not always work that way. I remember that growing up, the church my dad pastored had an outreach program focused on street evangelism. Every time they would go out into the local parks or neighborhoods and speak to people about Christ, it seemed our church would grow. The unique part of this is that my dad would always say that, more often than not, the people visiting our church were not the people the evangelism team encountered. I learned from this that the more my dad's church invested in The Kingdom, the more the church seemed to grow.

Many people, even leaders, would question this today and argue that the investment was not connected to the return. I would disagree with them; the Kingdom of God is everywhere, and where we invest does not matter so much as we do it.
I have found that over the years, God is still at work during the waiting process. Just because we see nothing taking place through our carnal eyes does not mean God is idle. Take, for instance, these four things:

1. God is renewing you. Titus 3:5 mentions the "renewing of the Holy Spirit," we can be thankful that He offers such a blessing. He does not anoint us once and then leaves us to live on one jar of oil. The Spirit sends fresh anointing when we are tired, poured out, or discouraged. He opens up bottles of new wine and fills us with new joy.
2. God is rebuilding you. Just as Nehemiah rebuilt the ruined city of Jerusalem, the Holy Spirit reconstructs your life. Nehemiah means "Comforter," a name Jesus used to describe the Spirit. You are under construction, and He has strategically placed orange cones and roadblocks in areas of your life.
3. God is refining you. The Holy Spirit is a fire, and He wants to burn up anything that does not resemble Christ. Like a smelter of gold, He melts us, skims off the toxic alloys, and melts us again to remove all impurities.
4. He is revealing His glory in and through you. The apostle Paul reminded us that because we have the Spirit inside us, we are now beholding the glory of the Lord "as in a mirror."

The result is that we "are being transformed into the same image from glory to glory." Don't focus on your flaws. Fix your eyes on Jesus. When you focus on yourself, you will be disappointed; when you focus on Him, you will be transformed.

The fact that God works on us during the waiting process can be found even in scripture. God may be preparing you for what he promised. Take King David, for example. We know that he was one of the most prolific kings of Israel, but do we know how he became king? He was just a young shepherd boy whom God gave a promise. God told David that he would become the next king through Samuel, the prophet. But it took many years. Why? God had to prepare David so that when he became king, he knew how to be a king.

This could be the exact reason why you are waiting. God wants to prepare you for what he promised before allowing you to enter it. He will take you into a new season once he knows you're ready. He is a good Father who does not set his children up for failure. He wants to give us good things, but only when we are ready. Now, here's the thing. It's your responsibility to submit to him and let him prepare you. If you resist what God is doing in this season, you set yourself up for failure in the next. Stay where God has placed you until he says you can move forward.

Perhaps you're waiting because God wants to show you how the Kingdom works. Good gifts from God take time. Like seeds, they need care and attention. The gift God wants to give you is too good to be made in a microwave. God wants us to press into his presence and wait patiently before his throne. He's calling us to come before him with thanksgiving, even if we are still waiting on a promise. The world has many things they want to offer us on an instantaneous silver platter. But good God-sent blessings take time.

NOTES

Date:

NOTES

Date:

NOTES

Date:

CHAPTER 5: THE HARVEST

Can you believe it? You're finally here, the moment that you have been waiting for. The moment when you reap all that you have sown—that's right, your "season" has arrived. As this time in your life unfolds, it will no doubt be filled with joy and anticipation. For some, these seasons take months to arrive, and for others, it is years, but no matter the amount of time spent waiting, harvest time is very special.

One unique point I want to highlight is the difference between "reap" and "harvest." There is little difference between harvest and reap. Both accomplish getting the reward of your labor from the plant into your hands for either selling, consuming, or giving to someone. The fundamental difference between harvest and reap is how the vegetables or fruits are taken from the plants. The word "reap" means using mechanical means to remove the product from the plant. Usually, the entire plant is damaged or completely destroyed.

On the other hand, the word "harvest" is to use one's hands to pick the produce. Harvest is a more "tender loving care" approach. Regardless of how it is done, one major thing they have in common is that harvesting and reaping both occur in the field. I cannot begin to count all the times I have heard people say, "It's my season" or "It's time for me to reap all I've sown." The reality is that reaping involves just as much work as sowing. Reaping or harvesting requires labor and, therefore, requires laborers. In Matthew 9:37, Jesus states, *"Then saith he unto his disciples, The harvest is plenteous, but the labourers are few."*

*Je*sus explained to his disciples that even though plenty of people needed the Gospel, the number of people willing to spread it was not plentiful. If I were to put it in my terms as a pastor, I would say that while the fields of the Kingdom are full, everyone is not willing to get in the field and work. To build the Kingdom of God, we must be willing workers and invest in people; after all, that is sowing. One key element of spiritual sowing is a physical investment in a person's life. This investment may be financial, it may be social, it may be simply being a friend or allowing them to express themselves.

Sometimes, doing good feels like a burden. I may already have too much on my emotional plate and not want to do anything more for the neighbor. Preparing a meal for someone who is sick might not be my forte. It might seem impossible to smile at others when I am hurting inside. Yet these actions are planting seeds that will eventually reap a harvest.

I know it is frustrating to work just as hard in your "due season" as you did when you were in the sowing process. I have been frustrated. I have been the leader who was wearing not just multiple hats but seemingly all of them. Remember the first day my wife and I began pastoring the congregation, which was less than ten people. It took six to eight months to form what many would call a "launch team." At the end of the first year of pastoral ministry, my wife and I were doing 90 percent of the work, and we were at only about 20 people.

During that second year, it was hard at times to remain steadfast. I had big ideas and a clear plan, but my wife and I had to attack most of it solo. This solo attack was not limited to just our physical efforts; it required financial effort as well.

Remember that when we launched in 2018, there were less than one thousand dollars in the church bank account.

A great deal of personal sowing had to take place for me to begin to see the "harvest" in our ministry. I noticed the growth at about the eighteen-month mark, November of 2019. For the first time as Pastor, I could see the beginning of the harvest season. As we entered 2020, our growth in multiple areas had increased, and as a Pastor or leader, you have to be able to recognize growth in various areas. Our church even now focuses on three primary areas of growth: Spiritual, Physical, and Financial.

As all of you may recall, things changed quickly in 2020 when COVID-19 occurred. There is no instruction manual for pastoring during a pandemic, and I can assure you that it was not covered in the seminary. This was uncharted territory, and as a Pastor, I was responsible for navigating the ministry through this difficult time.

Imagine my frustration, seeing growth and real progress for the first time, knowing that all these ideas were taking shape. Then boom, the Governor says that we cannot assemble. I was worried I would get phone calls from friends and hear stories of churches shrinking by 20 and 30 percent. This is where the testimony comes in for me; during COVID-19, our church grew. Not only was there spiritual and financial growth but there was also numerical growth. The first Sunday we were back in person, we had more people that day than any the previous year. In fact, by the end of 2020, we had grown by over 50 percent and were now consistently at 40 people.

Many of the things discussed during vision casting before the pandemic were still accomplished during the pandemic.
We had planned a sanctuary remodel. During the weeks that the building was "closed," I was able to get more work done and accomplish the goal faster. Another aspect of our vision casting was a small project to improve our foyer and make the "first impression" when people entered our building more appealing. This project was accomplished in less than two weeks simply because the building was unused.

In 2021, we entered the next phase of vision casting. We had a need to expand as our youth ministry experienced growth in 2021. The fact that we had maintained financially in 2020 in spite of the pandemic had set us up and made this project possible. This project is a new multi-purpose building, construction began early in 2022 and will be finished later this year.

As I approach year five as Lead Pastor, I think there were times when it seemed that I and the ministry were stuck in neutral. It took time for me to recognize that we were genuinely reaping a harvest and that God was blessing us. As a young leader, it can be hard to remain patient and trust that the work you are putting in is truly making an impact. The process of harvesting is not always smooth. There can be setbacks.
Nonetheless, keep expecting a harvest and nurturing until the job is done. Jesus was patient with those who were seeking God. We need to do the same.

Getting to the point of reaping a harvest is hard work. Let me encourage you not to be disappointed when it takes longer than you expect. Instead, be faithful to plant and nurture the seeds you plant in others, and always remember there is plenty of work to be done in the fields of the Kingdom.

NOTES

Date:

NOTES

Date:

NOTES

Date:

NOTES

Date:

NOTES

Date:

NOTES

Date:

NOTES

Date:

NOTES

Date:

NOTES

Date:

NOTES

NOTES

Date:

NOTES

Date:

NOTES

Date:

NOTES

NOTES

Date:

NOTES

Date:

NOTES

Date:

STAY CONNECTED

 charlesbatemanbooks

 canthonybateman@gmail.com

www.ingramcontent.com/pod-product-compliance
Lightning Source LLC
LaVergne TN
LVHW061601070526
838199LV00077B/7138